A Pictorial History
of the periodicals of the
Cumberland Presbyterian Church

By Dusty Luthy

Memphis, Tennessee
2021

Published by the Communications Ministry Team, CPC, and distributed by Cumberland Presbyterian Resources of the Discipleship Ministry Team, CPC.

The Communications Ministry Team of the Ministry Council of the Cumberland Presbyterian Church is the successor organization to the Board of the Cumberland Presbyterian Magazine of the Cumberland Presbyterian Church.

Funded, in part, by your contributions to Our United Outreach.

First Edition 2021

ISBN: 978-1-945929-26-7

A Pictorial History
of the periodicals of the
Cumberland Presbyterian Church

This publication is dedicated to all those who have contributed in word, photo, or subscription to the "official publication" of the Cumberland Presbyterian denomination — *The Cumberland Presbyterian*. You have made our denomination's history and future so much more meaningful.

Special thanks to Susan Gore and Missy Rose for their assistance in the archives.

And especial kudos to Dr. Barry Anderson, Dr. Jay Earheart-Brown, Dr. Lee Ramsey, Dr. Pete Gathje, and Dr. Andy McClung at Memphis Theological Seminary who allowed me space to creatively fulfill final assigment obligations in manners such as this.

Bound copies of the Cumberland Presbyterian housed at the library of Memphis Theological Seminary in Memphis, Tenn.

Picture It...

As Samuel McAdow, Samuel King, and Finis Ewing sat around a wood stove in a log cabin in February 1810, praying, talking, and discerning, the printed word was on their minds.

The three Presbyterian ministers, guided by matters of the Holy Spirit and deep conviction, were guided not only by a book called the Bible, but also one called the Westminster Confession of Faith. In the latter, doctrines regarding interpretations of the scriptures held in the Bible gave the ministers, and many others, reason for concern and pause.

While McAdow, King, and Ewing didn't set out to create a new denomination that night in February, printed words helped guide their hearts to a new path for a group of people called Cumberland Presbyterians for the next 200-plus years.

Even though at the time of the fateful log cabin night, paper was still made from cotton pulp rather than wood pulp[1], printed words, especially through the publication of periodicals, would become one of the key ways Cumberland Presbyterians, and other Christians, would communicate news, theology, encouragement, and entertainment to one another.

BIRTHPLACE SHRINE
February 4, 1810

Finis Ewing's **Lectures** *were theological discussions surrounding the new Cumberland theology.*

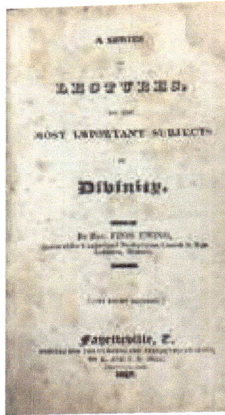

Early Publications of the Cumberland Presbyterian Church

Before any official mandate or publishing house, Cumberland Presbyterians were actively publishing and proliferating spiritual reading materials, including articles and pamphlets, from the very beginning.[2]

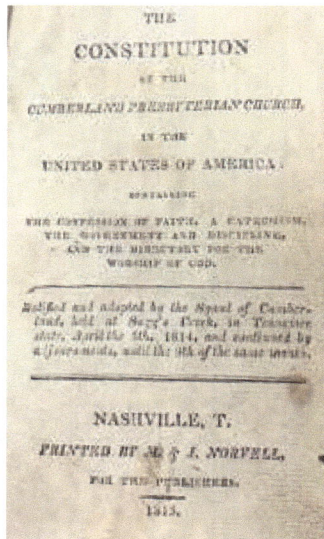

By 1814, the Cumberland Synod authorized the creation of a new Confession of Faith to replace the Westminster Confession, which Cumberlands were using despite their objections to predestination. The first Cumberland Confession was printed in 1815.

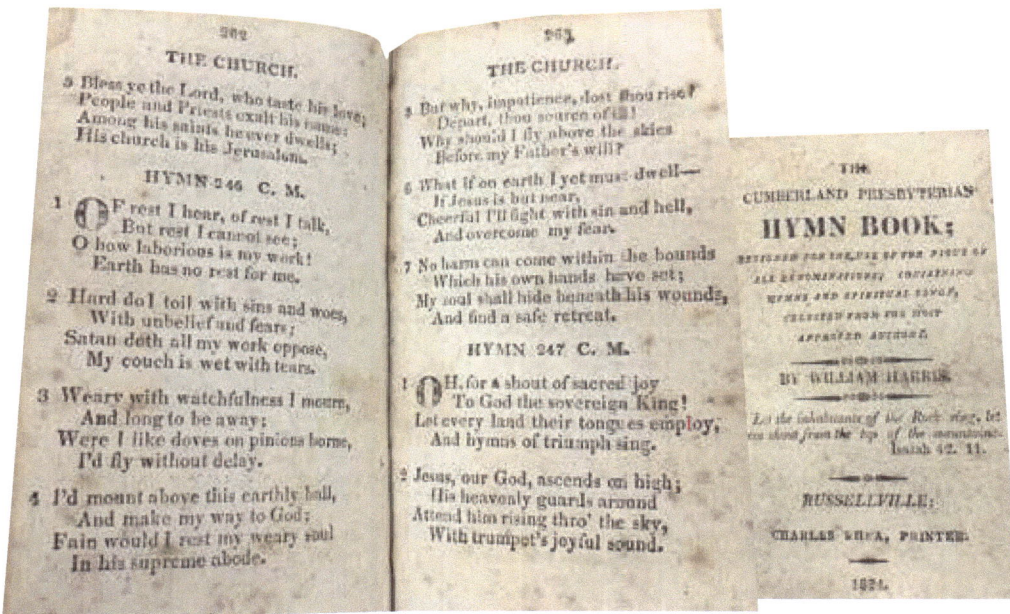

Cumberland Presbyterians were also circulating a hymn book — but don't look for musical notes if you find a copy! Hymns were listed by tune, and sung in "common meter" which would have been tunes familiar to people of the time and reused for different hymn wordings.

F.R. Cossitt and Cumberland College

It took barely fifteen years for the Cumberland Presbyterians to begin their first educational opportunities, settling on establishing Cumberland College in 1825 in Princeton, Kentucky. Franceway Ranna Cossitt was named the school's first president. The college was the catalyst for the Cum-berland Presbyterian Publishing House, a natural exten-sion of the intellectual and educational mission of the school.[3]

F.R. Cossitt, who had entertained thoughts about beginning a newspaper in 1822,[4] was gaining prestige in his travels, preaching, and other small pamphlet publishing ventures, and through the college, began the denomina-tion's first periodical, the **Religious and Literary Intelli-gencer,** in 1830. That same year, the General Assembly adopted the paper as an official mission of the church, overseeing its publication and naming Rev. David Lowry as editor after serving as Cossitt's assistant.[5]

F.R. Cossitt

In 1930, the **Religious and Literary In-telligencer** published weekly at a cost of $2.00 per year with any possible net prof-its benefiting Cumberland College.[6] A typ-ical edition of the paper included religious news from around the state and the world, presbytery and synod news, letters from readers, poetry, and advertising.

David Lowry

"Devoted to Religion, Literature, Science, Agriculture and General Intelligence."
     - **Religious and Literary Intelligencer** motto

Religious and Literary INTELLIGENCER.

DEVOTED TO RELIGION, LITERATURE, SCIENCE, AGRICULTURE AND GENERAL INTELLIGENCE.

EDITED AND PUBLISHED BY REV. DAVID LOWRY.—A. BROCK, PRINTER.

NUMBER 35.   PRINCETON, KY. DECEMBER 9, 1830.   VOLUME I.

ECCLESIASTICAL.

MINUTES OF THE FRANKLIN SYNOD.

MEMBERS PRESENT.

CHRISTIANITY.

REPORT

Of the committee appointed by the Franklin Synod to examine into the state of religion within her bounds.

RICHARD BEARD, *Moderator.*
John L. Barns, *Clerk.*

JOHN L. DILLARD, *Chairman.*
Wm. H. Boyle, *Clerk.*

ON THE SPIRIT OF FORGIVENESS.

ROBERT C. DUNLAP.

SUNDAY SCHOOL DEPARTMENT.

VINDEX.

MINISTERS' DEPARTMENT.

Controversy With Early Publications

Two years after its humble beginnings, the de-nominational paper moved to Nashville, Tennessee, from Princeton, Kentucky, in 1832, and changed its name to the *Revivalist*.[7]

A year later, the paper was sold to Rev. James Smith, who in 1834 changed the name to *Cum-berland Presbyterian*. The paper struggled fi-nancially at this time.[8]

In 1839, a denominational committee moved the paper's publishing duties to Lebanon, Tennessee, and named Rev. George Donnell as editor.[9]

But Smith wasn't quite ready to relinquish his ed-itor duties. A few months after the move, Smith resumed printing and distribution of a publication in September 1839 from Springfield, Tennessee.[10]

F. R. Cossitt even joined back in the game, cre-ating an entirely new publication in 1840 called *The Banner of Peace*.[11]

For the next 34 years, a plethora of publications proliferated — and most fizzled.

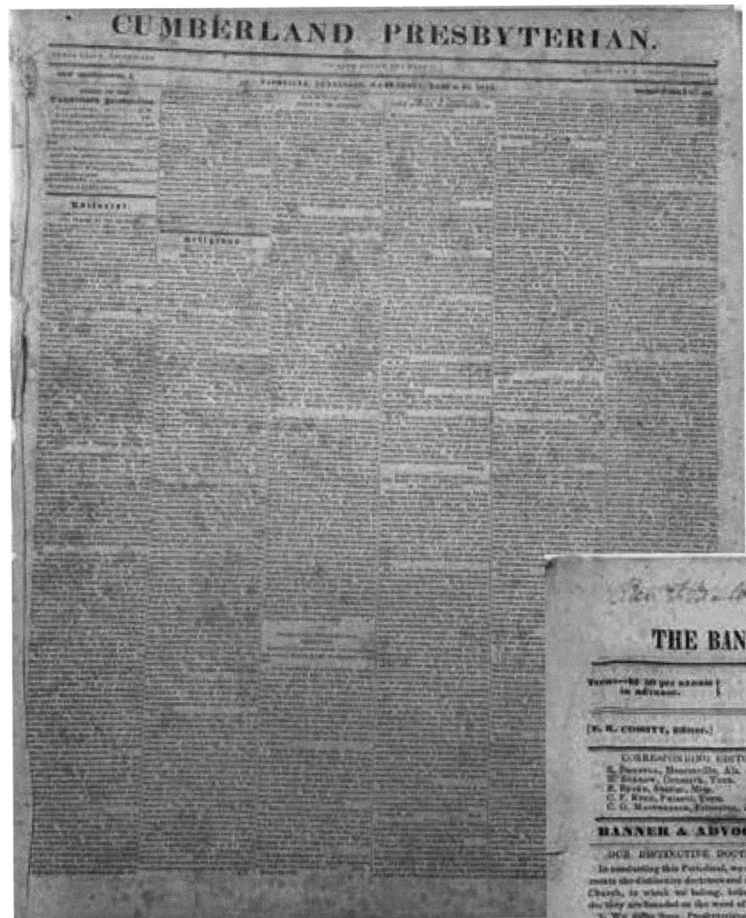

List of private publications published in the interest of the church

■ *Cumberland Presbyterian Pulpit* - published by James Smith in Nashville, Tennessee, beginning in 1833, and lasted about two years.
■ *The Banner of Peace* - established by F.R. Cossitt in 1840, endured a succession of owners, editors, and publishing locations, eventually folding and selling its subscription list to the Board of Publications in 1874.
■ *Union and Evangelist* - began in 1840 by John Morgan in Uniontown, Pennsylvania, and taken over by Milton Bird upon Morgan's death in 1841. Lasted through various changes in names, (including a change to *Cumberland Presbyterian*) editors, and locations, until its subscription list was sold to J.B. Logan who published a paper in Alton, Illinois.

■ *The Ark* - established in 1841, and combined with the *Banner of Peace* in 1850
■ *The Texas Presbyterian* - published in four different locations throughout Texas from 1846 to about 1856
■ *Watchman and Evangelist* - begun by Milton Bird, and eventually combined with the *Missouri Cumberland Presbyterian* in 1858 to form the *St. Louis Observer*.
■ *The Ladies' Pearl* - established in 1852 by W. S. Langdon and J.C. Provine in Nashville, Tennessee., and eventually sold and published in Alton, Illinois, but published continuously through 1884.
■ *Missouri Cumberland Presbyterian* - began in Lexington, Missouri, in 1852, and combined with the *Watch-*man and Evangelist in 1858 to create the *St. Louis Observer*.

■ *St. Louis Observer* - formed in 1858 with the combination of the *Watchman and Evangelist* and the *Mis-souri Cumberland Presbyterian* with Milton Bird its first editor
■ *The Theological Medium* - began by Milton Bird in 1845, but ceased publication after several different names and publishing cities in the late 1850s
■ *The Presbyter* - established by T.M. Johnston at Alamo, Calif., in 1860, and changed its name to the *Pacific Cum-*

James Smith

Milton Bird

Board of Publications

The denominational Board of Publications was first created in 1845 after General Assembly adopted resolutions from 1843 with mixed results.

A separate committee was created in 1847 and merged into the board, with Rev. Mil-ton Bird becoming secretary, publishing agent, book editor, and salesman in an endeavor termed the "Book Concern" by an early biographer. Publica-tions were based at this time in Lou sville, Kentucky.[12] Bird had a few years prior, taken over publishing duties of the *Union Evangelist* and began sever-al other periodicals during his time on the board, although spor sored individually and not denominationally.[13]

As with other individual pub-lishing endeavors, continued mismanagement condemned the ledgling board. A 1858 audit found that about 30,000 volumes of materials had been been printed by the board in a four year period, mostly in the form of hymn books and Con-fessions of Faith, with little re-turn in revenue.[14]

The committee was reconsti-tuted in 1858 and moved to Nashville.[15]

Publishing work of the church was largely suspended during the Civil War until 1863 when it transferred to Pittsburgh.[16]

The board, and the denomi-national publications, moved back to Nashville in 1867.[17]

In 1872, the board purchased the *Theological Medium* and the *Sunday School Gem* from individuals to become denominationally supported publications.[18]

Up to this point, the Board of Publications had no publishing rights over any periodicals.

Publications of the Cumber-land Presbyterian denomina-tion in 1858:

- ■ Hymn Book
- ■ Social Harp
- ■ Confession of Faith
- ■ Manual
- ■ Ewing's Lectures
- ■ Donnell's Thoughts
- ■ Guide to Infant Baptism
- ■ Infant Philosophy
- ■ A Commentary on the Sixth Chapter of Hebrews

berland Presbyterian and then to the *Pacif-ic Observer.* Sold in 1871, and published in San Francisco for a short time
- ■ *The American Presbyterian and East Tennessee Cumberland* - began in 1851 with J.B. Dobson as editor
- ■ *Texas Medium* - published in 1852
- ■ *Texas Pulpit* - edited by James Samp-son, James Guthrie, and M. Priest in 1851.

— *A People Called Cumberland Presbyterian,*
p. 239-240

The General Assembly Mandate

Even though the General Assembly in 1858 had expressed interest in consolidating the denominational publications, it wasn't until later conditions existed to make the goal a reality.[19] 1874 was a big year for Cumberland Presbyterian publications. At the time, a Board of Publications existed, and a separate standing Committee on Publications discussed the board report and explored repeated requests for an official church paper.

Because the issue was such an important one of the day, the standing rules of the meeting included the direction that this was to be the special order, and that all who had an opinion on the matter would be permitted to speak.[20]

The committee began by presenting its report on the fifth day of the assembly, spending several hours in discussion before being adjourned for the next day. On day six, Wednesday, publications was still the topic of the day, and the report wasn't amended and adopted until that afternoon.[21]

The assembly agreed, at the request of the Board of Publication, to establish and back a weekly church paper, and go so far as to buy out the top three pre-existing regional denominational weekly publications.[22]

Three publications merged into one:
Banner of Peace, Cumberland Presbyterian, Texas Cumberland Presbyterian

The first proposed name was **Banner-Presbyterian**, but due to its lack of popularity, the **Cumberland Presbyterian** reigned.[23]

Total cost to purchase three publications and their subscription lists:

$25,500[24]

(or $572,178.03 in 2018)

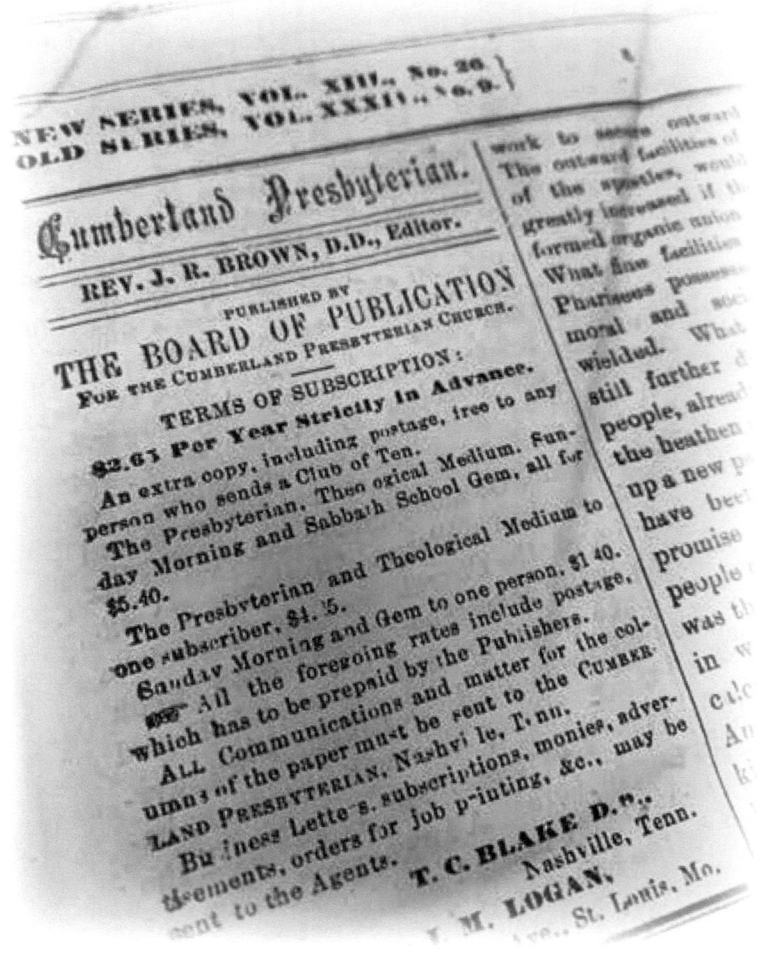

"It furnishes about twice as much reading matter as any one of its predecessors. It has grown steadily in influence and usefulness. Thus the church has one large weekly to which all our people can justly look with satisfaction — strong, able, and under the church's own control."

- Rev. B.W. McDonnold, *History of the Cumberland Presbyterian Church*

Purpose and function of periodicals

First and foremost, the denominational publication's main purpose was to help the "cause of Christianity."[25] A periodical allowed not only information and news to be shared, but theology, inspiration, and direction for ministry.

Milton L. Baughn, a Cumberland Presbyterian historian, notes that the content of the *Cumberland Presbyterian* reflected the opinions of the editor at the time of publication, rather than the consensus of readers or the denomination as a whole.[26] For decades after the birth of the denomination, the Cumberland Church saw systemic injustices such as slavery, as social issues and not as religious issues, and refused to get involved.[27]

At times, moral and social issues such as temperance and Sabbath became topics of editorials. A decade before the turn of the 20th century, however, while the paper refused to take a side in party politics, voicing opinions against lynching and advocating for election reform was becoming more common.[28]

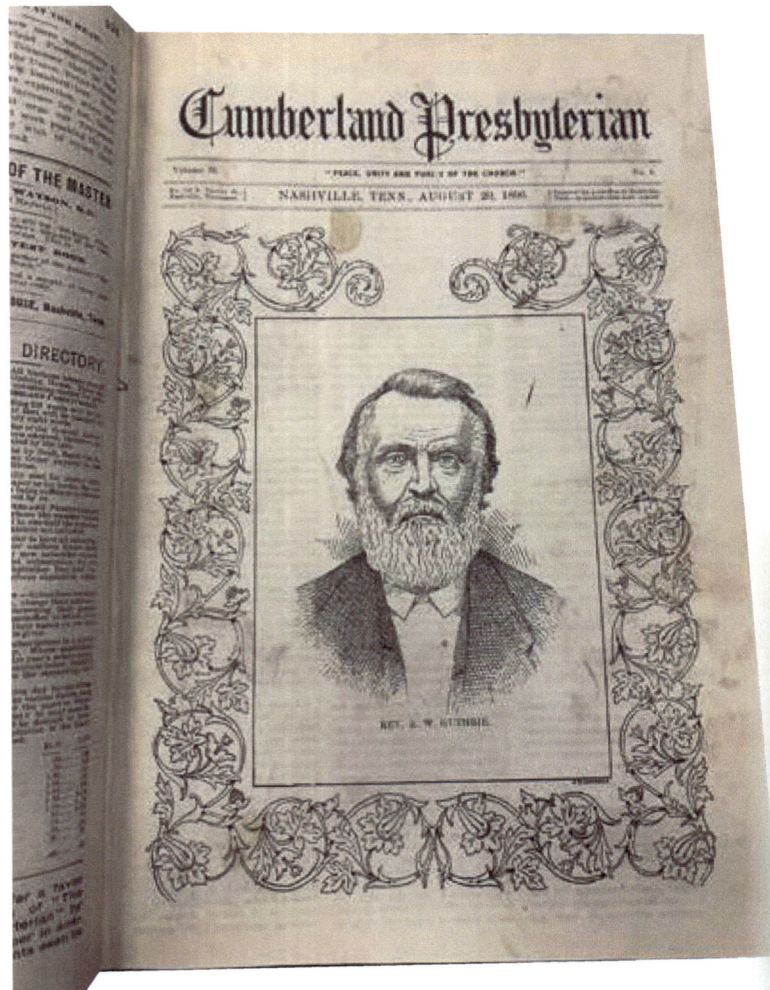

"Your Committee commend the cause of Publication to the whole Church, invoking its patronage and its enlightened liberality, believing that there is no greater auxiliary to the propagation of truth and the permanent establishment of the cause of Christianity."

- Publications Committee report in 1874 minutes of the General Assembly

Biblical Scriptures on Drinking

By Rev. W. A. Smith in Alabama Baptist

Too long we have listened to that pious expression coming from many quarters which says, "Let the preacher stay with the Bible, and leave the liquor question with the laymen and politicians." One has only to examine the Bible to find it full of references condemning the drink evil. In fact, if the preacher is to preach the whole truth, and be fair with the word of God, he must preach against this sin.

I have taken Young's concordance and other helps, and have made a study of the Bible on the subject. It is revealing indeed. Here one finds scores of direct references, comprising 162 verses of Scriptures. This is more Scripture than one will find on any of the subjects of lying, adultery, swearing, stealing, Sabbath-breaking, cheating, hypocrisy, pride, or even blasphemy.

12. II Sam. 11: 13. Only by strong drink could David lead Uriah into the trap which cost him his life.

13. I Kings 16: 8-10. While a king was "drinking himself drunk" in his own house, one of his captains conspired against him and slew him.

14. I Kings 20: 13-21. No drinking army can hope to win battles. While Benhadad and thirty-two other kings were "drinking themselves drunk" in their pavilions, a small band of Israel's men fell upon the Syrians and put them to flight.

15. Esther 1: 22. Drink wrecks homes and causes separation of man and wife. At a drinking party which lasted a week, King Ahasuerus, while drunk, subjected his queen to the beastly gaze of drunken nobles and thus brought on the separation of king and queen.

"Peace, Unity and Purity of the Church."

- 19th century *Cumberland Presbyterian* motto

Early Content

Early church papers functioned not only to give members of the denomination church news, but local, regional, and world news, as well as commodities updates.

Financing the Church

JULY BUDGET OFFERING

TOTAL FOR JULY	$1,287.25
Last Year for July	749.42
INCREASE OVER LAST YEAR	537.83
GRAND TOTAL THIS YEAR	$3,125.37
Last Year to date	2,610.58
Total Increase for May, June and July	514.79

MEANING OF THE DENOMINATIONAL BUDGET

Every denomination faces the problem of financing certain agencies which are charged with the responsibility of promoting the denominational program. In the Cumberland Presbyterian Church, there are seven agencies and boards which must be financed in order to do the work and carry out the program of the General Assembly. Prior to 1924 these agencies were financed by gifts, drives for money, special days, special appeals, and other money-raising methods that became an unpleasant aspect of the Church's financial policies. The Church felt new standards of giving should be set up, a new attitude toward money created, and a new way of financing the denomination's work instituted. Such

The Cumberland Presbyterian. 25

nation to organize a systematic, well-developed tithing program carrying with it the endorsement of the highest court of the Church. The first tithing program was the result of a vision of Hon. Vint N. Bray, about 1915. Later the tithing and budget programs were so planned and organized that they could be worked in conjunction with each other—the one to aid the other. A committee composed of one from each of several boards was appointed to superintend the tithing and budget campaign. Hon. Frank McDonald was the first secretary-treasurer and general director appointed by the General Assembly.

The Board of Tithing and Budget, as a board, brought its first report to the General Assembly in 1924. Various individuals have served faithfully on the board and in the field in a conceivable effort to make adequate to the needs of any agencies. Everyone served is to be commended had a part in the gradual of the program, which it is believed will eventually solve cial problems of the Chu possible the raising of budget. The history of t

By Rev. Wayne Wiman
Send all budget money to Rev. Wayne Wiman, 602 Empire Building, Memphis, Tennessee.

home office while the field man in his visitation preached sermons on tithing and took personal as well as congregational pledges to the budget.

For a time there was a separate secretary for the tithing department of the board, whose work was later combined with that of the general secretary.

In 1929, the field man's services were discontinued and the key-man plan instituted with a secretary-treasurer in a home office.

From 1930 to 1933, in addition to and continuing the key-man plan, a budget field man was employed with a board secretary in a home office. The field man drove thousands of miles personally contacting churches and enrolling tithers.

The CUMBERLAND PRESBYTERIAN

IN ESSENTIALS UNITY, IN NON-ESSENTIALS LIBERTY, AND IN ALL THINGS CHARITY

NASHVILLE, TENN., AUGUST 22, 1941

New East Side, Memphis, Church

November 26, 1896.

Our Church News.

SOME REASONS FOR DENOMINATIONAL THANKSGIVING.

MANCHESTER, Tenn.—Rev. J. W. Simmons has been here one year. During the time there have been 60 additions to the church. A neat 6-room parsonage has been erected and is now occupied.

MERIDIAN, Miss.—Evangelist W. M. Robison, of Marshall, Texas, lately held a two-weeks' meeting here to the great benefit of the church. The Christian Endeavorers did valiant service during the meeting. Rev. R. A. Cody is pastor.

DENISON, Texas.—Rev. E. H. Liles closed his second year's pastorate here Oct. 1. During the time he has received 28 members, 24 the past year. The Honey Grove congregation has lately contributed $50 in cash and pledges for this mission. Rev. A. L. Barr, pastor at Honey Grove, says this amount will be increased to $100. Mrs. E. E. Moody, widow of the late pastor here, Rev. E. E. Moody, has returned to make her home with her mother at Denison.

"In essentials unity; in non-essentials liberty, and in all things charity."
- 20th century **Cumberland Presbyterian** motto

Periodicals and Propaganda

Periodicals became a breeding ground for propaganda regarding the possible union with the mother Presbyterian Church. While the union actually occurred in 1906, articles in the Cumberland Presbyterian as early as 1896 planted the seeds of discord and disunity — or possibility and practicality, if that was your persuasion.[29]

Rev. Ira Landrith, a chief unionist, was the editor of **The Cumberland Presbyterian**, the denominational voice, during the important years of discussion and disagreement. Landrith would go on to be the moderator during the 1906 General Assembly that adjourned and effectively dissolved the church. Rev. James E. Clarke was the editor of **The Cumberland Presbyterian** at the time of the merger.

Two denominationally unsupported publications, **The Cumberland Banner** and **The Cumberland Evangel,** merged after a conference in 1904 in St. Louis whose sole purpose was to discuss unification with the mother church — and to oppose it.[30] Joseph Fussell, a judge and an elder in the church, protested the union continually, and often provided articles in the new publication.

In fact, in this new publication, also called **The Cumberland Banner,** an editorial insisted that the "denominational organ, **The Cumberland Presbyterian,** has published a report of the St. Louis conference that is in a serious measure a perversion of its spirit and a garbled account of the proceedings. Some of the participants in that conference are made to say things that they did not say. The best way to dispose of this report as published in our denominational paper of the 7th inst. is a repudiation of the whole."[31]

Information, fact or fiction, was not for want during this period of time.

Joseph Fussell

"Oh, no, the united church is not heaven, but neither is unnecessarily divided Presbyterianism. Brethren, let's be careful about our threats. More than one good and wise opponent of union has come to believe that this movement is of God; and it would be sad if they had been of those who vowed that they would never, never, never unite."

—Rev. Ira Landrith - editorial,
The Cumberland Presbyterian,
Oct. 6, 1904

Ira Landrith

The 1906 Union

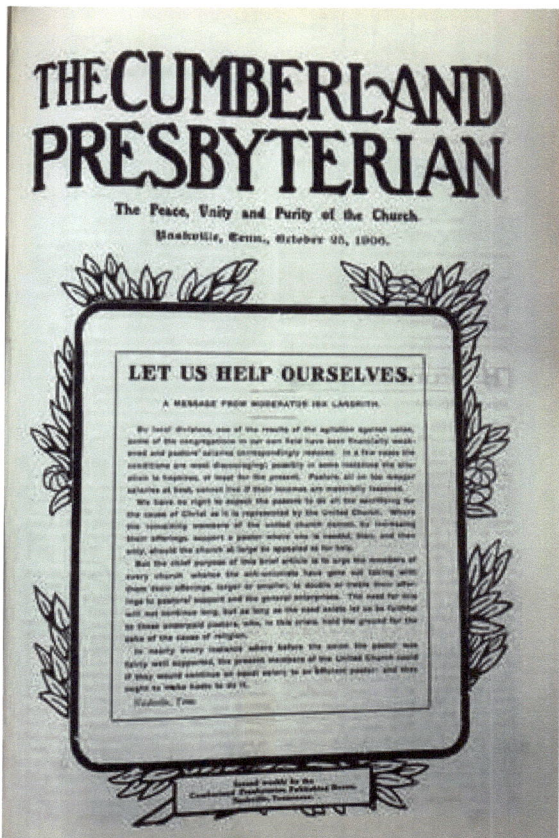

Following the union of Cumberland Presbyterians with the Presbyterians, *The Cumberland Presbyterian* periodical continued to publish — in the hands of the unionists. Content included updates on the union, particular legal issues regarding court decisions and challenges faced with the union holdouts, who continued the Cumberland Presbyterian denomination. Of particular concern was the distribution and ownership of property.

Anti-unionists, who continued to connect through the publication, *The Cumberland Banner*, were still criticized as spreading harmful propaganda.

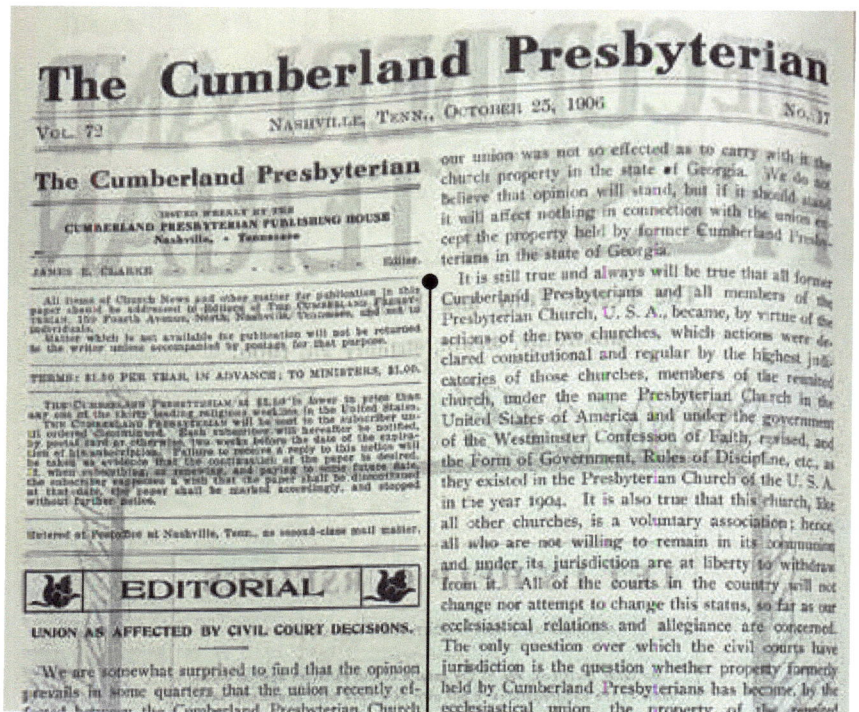

"*It is also true that this church, like all other churches, is a voluntary association; hence, all who aren't willing to remain in its communion and under its jurisdiction are at liberty to withdraw from it. .... The only question over which the civil courts have jurisdiction is the question whether property formerly held by Cumberland Presbyterians has become, by the ecclesiastical union, the property of the reunited church.*"

— Editorial,
The Cumberland Presbyterian,
Oct. 25, 1906

The Cumberland Presbyterian Comes Home

While denominational activities and functions changed following the 1906 union with the Presbyterian Church, the denominational voice was still in the hands of the unionists. Following legal battles and court settlements, *The Cumberland Presbyterian* came back to its roots with much celebration.

R.L. Baskette, in his book *History of Publication of the Cumberland Presbyterian Church*, harshly criticized the decade the newspaper was effectively held hostage by the partisan editors Ira Landrith and James Clarke. Baskette described the fallout from the union as "the awful wreck and ruin produced by the betrayal of our Church into the hands of the Presbyterian Church, U.S.A."[32]

In the first edition back in the hands of true Cumberland Presbyterians, published March 3, 1910, Clarke was sent off in an editorial where he was warmly praised for his work. But the writer didn't hesitate to poke a quick jab: "Yes, the retiring editor is dignified, he is a man of thought, he is courteous, but unfortunately he has forgotten how to express or pronounce the phrase 'The Cumberland Presbyterian Church,' which only a few years ago provided for him 'a rest in a weary land.' Editor Clarke forgets, he forgets, but doubtless consoles himself that it was all predestinated and foreordained, but he forgets!"[33]

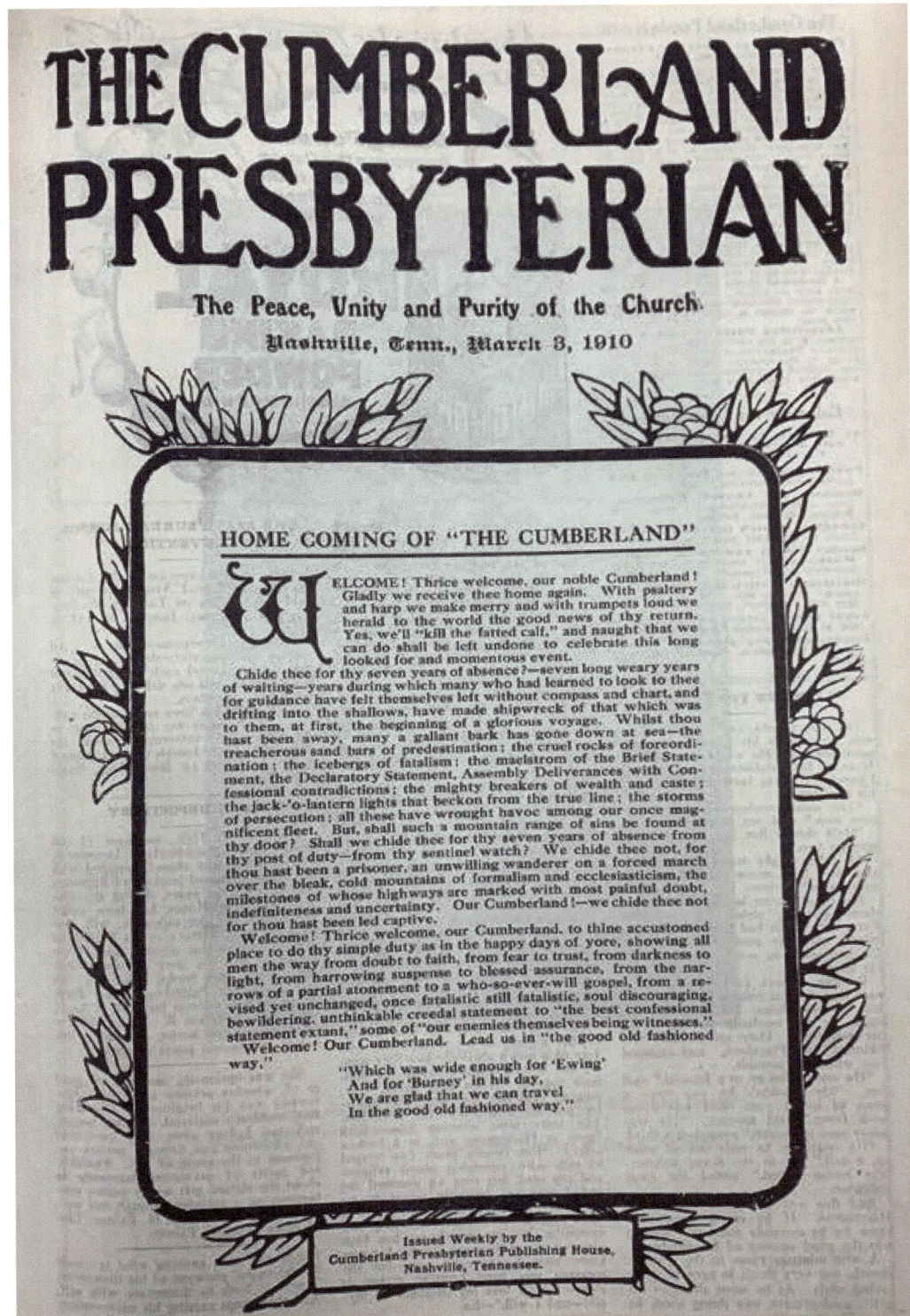

THE CUMBERLAND PRESBYTERIAN

The Peace, Unity and Purity of the Church.

Nashville, Tenn., March 3, 1910

HOME COMING OF "THE CUMBERLAND"

WELCOME! Thrice welcome, our noble Cumberland! Gladly we receive thee home again. With psaltery and harp we make merry and with trumpets loud we herald to the world the good news of thy return. Yes, we'll "kill the fatted calf," and naught that we can do shall be left undone to celebrate this long looked for and momentous event.

Chide thee for thy seven years of absence?—seven long weary years of waiting—years during which many who had learned to look to thee for guidance have felt themselves left without compass and chart, and drifting into the shallows, have made shipwreck of that which was to them, at first, the beginning of a glorious voyage. Whilst thou hast been away, many a gallant bark has gone down at sea—the treacherous sand bars of predestination; the cruel rocks of foreordination; the icebergs of fatalism; the maelstrom of the Brief Statement, the Declaratory Statement, Assembly Deliverances with Confessional contradictions; the mighty breakers of wealth and caste; the jack-'o-lantern lights that beckon from the true line; the storms of persecution; all these have wrought havoc among our once magnificent fleet. But, shall such a mountain range of sins be found at thy door? Shall we chide thee for thy seven years of absence from thy post of duty—from thy sentinel watch? We chide thee not, for thou hast been a prisoner, an unwilling wanderer on a forced march over the bleak, cold mountains of formalism and ecclesiasticism, the milestones of whose highways are marked with most painful doubt, indefiniteness and uncertainty. Our Cumberland!—we chide thee not for thou hast been led captive.

Welcome! Thrice welcome, our Cumberland, to thine accustomed place to do thy simple duty as in the happy days of yore, showing all men the way from doubt to faith, from fear to trust, from darkness to light, from harrowing suspense to blessed assurance, from the narrows of a partial atonement to a who-so-ever-will gospel, from a revised yet unchanged, once fatalistic still fatalistic, soul discouraging, bewildering, unthinkable creedal statement to "the best confessional statement extant," some of "our enemies themselves being witnesses." Welcome! Our Cumberland. Lead us in "the good old fashioned way."

"Which was wide enough for 'Ewing'
And for 'Burney' in his day,
We are glad that we can travel
In the good old fashioned way."

Issued Weekly by the
Cumberland Presbyterian Publishing House,
Nashville, Tennessee.

Other Publications

In the Cumberland Presbyterian church's 200-plus year history, publications have been standard fare for communications purposes. Some thrived. Some didn't survive. Some played an important role for their time in history, even if they didn't make it to the present. Some were published by individuals, some were part of the Board of Publications and official denominationally-sponsored means of communications.

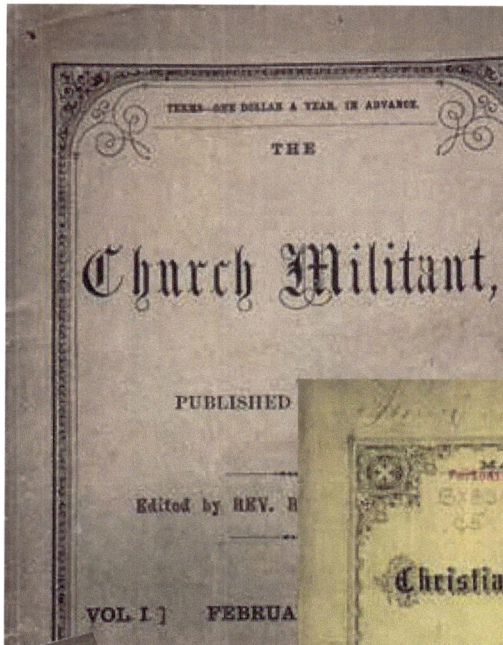

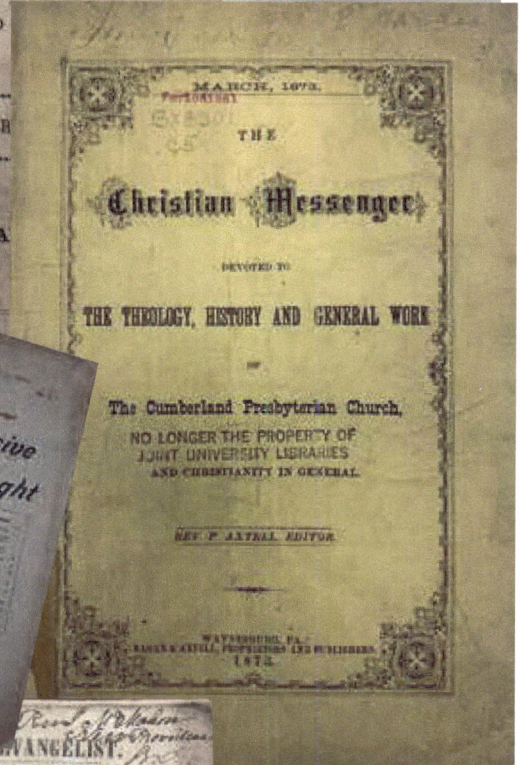

Editors of the Cumberland Presbyterian

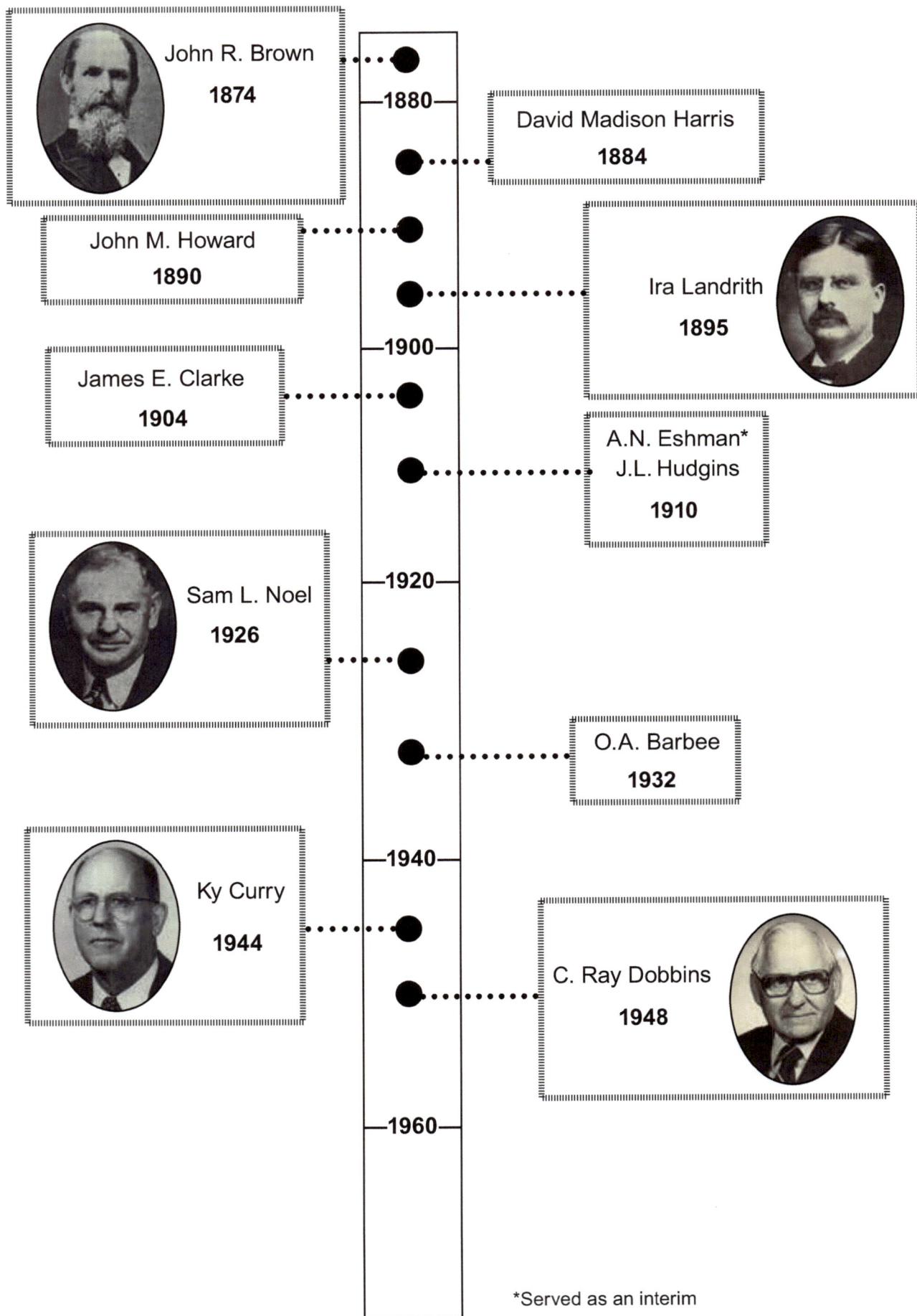

John R. Brown
1874

David Madison Harris
1884

John M. Howard
1890

Ira Landrith
1895

—1880—

—1900—

James E. Clarke
1904

A.N. Eshman*
J.L. Hudgins
1910

—1920—

Sam L. Noel
1926

O.A. Barbee
1932

—1940—

Ky Curry
1944

C. Ray Dobbins
1948

—1960—

*Served as an interim

—1980—

Richard Magrill
1984

Mark Brown#
1987

Pat White
2000

Harold Davis*
M. Jacqueline
DeBerry Warren
1993

—2000—

Mark Davis
2010

Matthew H. Gore
2018

—2020—

—2040—

*Served as an interim
Includes 2 years as interim

Editors of the Cumberland Presbyterian

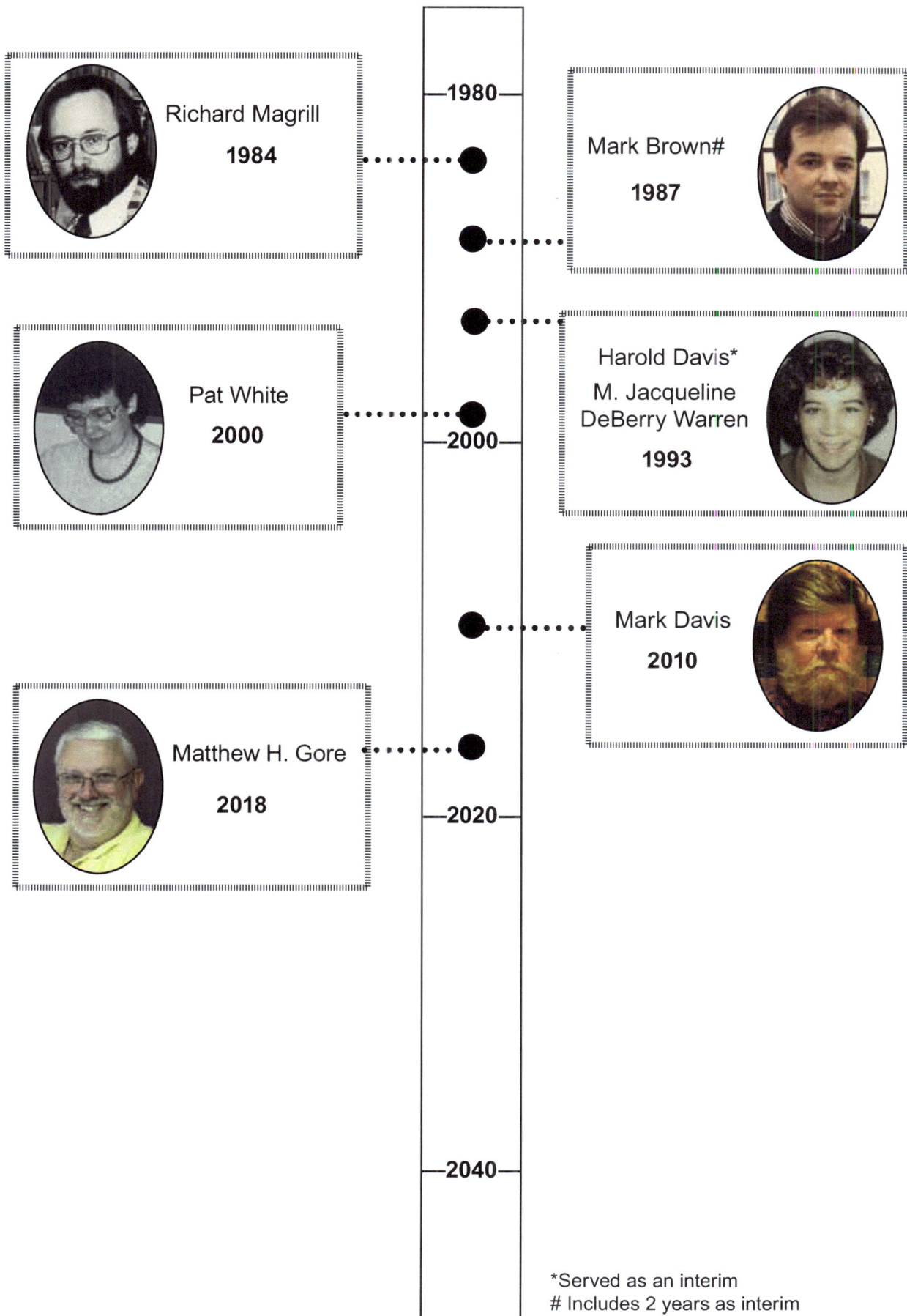

The Cumberland Presbyterian Flag

The Cumberland Flag is the official denominational publication of the Cumberland Presbyterian Church in America. First published in 1931, it has served as a key tool in sharing denominational news.

Prior to the **Flag**, the denomination circulated the **Colored Cumberland Presbyterian**, and various presbyteries and synods distributed local newsletters.[34]

Early Editors:

- Dr. W. D. Edington - 1931
- Rev. Dr. William Fowlkes - 1942
- Dr. Helen B. Nichols - 1973

Rev. William Fowlkes

"Peace, Truth, Righteousness."

- **Cumberland Flag** motto

"Among other things, the church paper has stimulated church interest, kept the constituency abreast of events concerning the general church as well as congregations of the denomination. Additionally, it has fostered church pride, served as a tool for education and community-building and it continues to serve those functions in 1981."

- as printed in January 1981 as *The Cumberland Flag* celebrated 50 years of publication

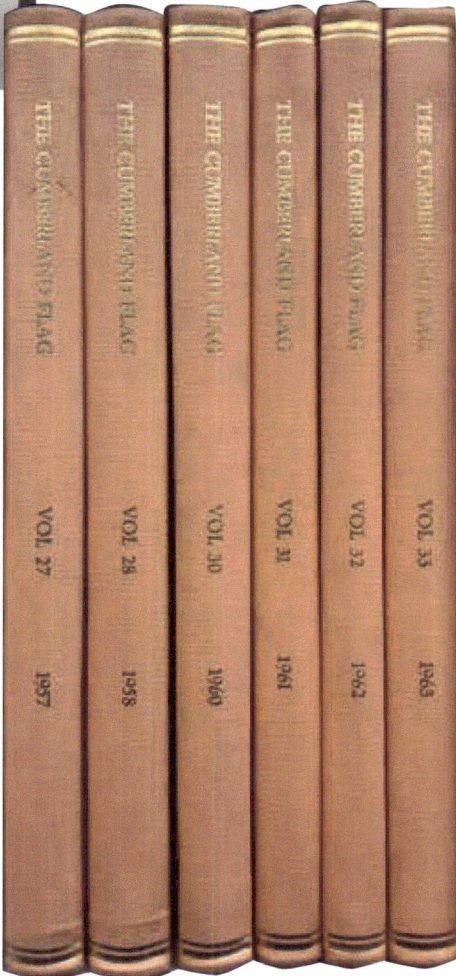

Missions Publications

Of particular interest to Cumberland Presbyterians, and Christians everywhere, was the proliferation of the gospel in the form of missionary efforts. By 1845, the denomination established the Board of Foreign and Domestic Missions to coordinate its missions efforts.

The backbone of missions efforts, however, came from a specific group. Cumberland Presbyterian women united and by 1880, coordinated their own Women's Board of Missions, going so far as to develop a constitution and receive General Assembly approval.

The first missions-focused publication began in 1851, and by the later part of the century,[35] at least one of the publications were produced by the Women's Board and included female editors. One of the most popular publications was the monthly *Missionary Banner,* which featured exotic photos and stories of faith work internationally.

A WOMAN OF INDIA.

"Now be the Gospel Banner, In every land unfurled, and be the shout 'Hosanna,' Reechoed through the world."

— *Missionary Banner* motto

Jubilee Journal

The Women's Board of Mission reorganized its publications efforts, and in January 1930, after much talk and promotion, began distributing the *Jubilee Journal* in honor of 50 years of successful and fruitful women's ministry mission efforts. Johnie Massey Clay, the much-beloved president of the Women's Board of Mission, was the publication's first editor. The purpose of the publication also served as a support for individual missionary societies — which would benefit from a streamlined message.[36]

Early issues boasted of 1,032 subscribers, and included content such as:

■ Updates on board members' health and status
■ Notes on China ministry by Gam Sing Quah
■ Devotionals
■ Responsive readings for society meetings

■ Mission ministry opportunities to better build the societies
■ Letters from Missionaries, including E.L. Conyers and Bernice Barnett

Johnie Massey Clay

"Women stronger grown. Thousands of them. Giving, giving, giving of love, self and time. Saner, truer and noble grown from following FIFTY YEARS in the WAY. It is the promise of HIM whom they follow. This also is the reward, the harvest, of FIFTY YEARS of seed-sowing. And all this is the true and full meaning of MISSIONS in the heart of men and women in the world."

— editorial,
Jubilee Journal
January 1930

Missionary Messenger

After a successful celebration of the jubilee year of women's ministry and foreign mission work, the missions publication received a quick redesign following the women's convention meeting in 1931. While the editors bemoaned the loss of the personal touches of hand drawings and the intimate writing styles, the new publication, **The Missionary Messenger,** became an official vehicle for missions updates from the field to the pews.[37]

Continuously published ever since, **The Missionary Messenger** originally began as a monthly periodical, but in 2012 became a quarterly publication. Gone are subscriptions; instead, the magazine is sent to every household in the Cumberland Presbyterian Church free of charge and made possible by funds from Our United Outreach.

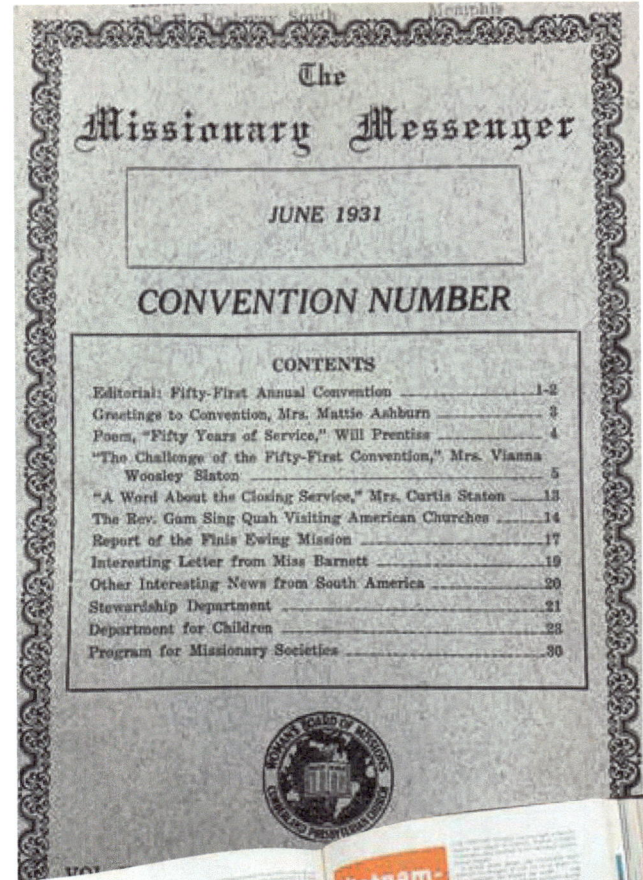

Missionary Messenger

Bridging the Past and the Present

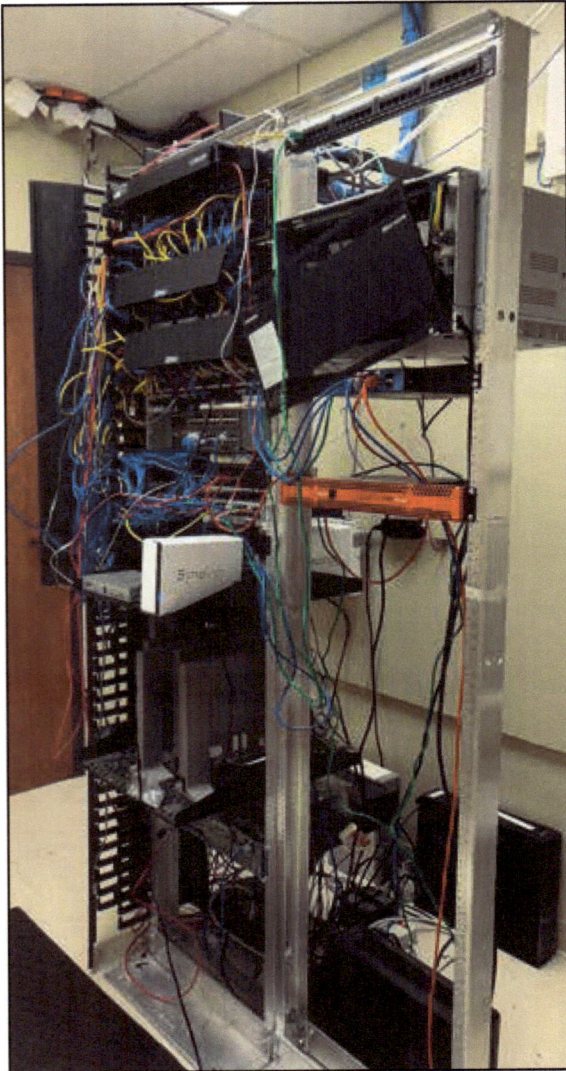

Wires, filled with information, fiber optics, and electricity, coupled with wireless devices that connect to the Internet, are the new wave of the future of communications. This tower, housed in its own special room in the Denominational Center in Memphis, Tennessee, connects those working at the center to telephones and the Internet.

More than 100 years have passed, and **The Cumberland Presbyterian**, now a full-fledged magazine, continues publication. It has gone through a variety of editors, published hundreds of articles, photos, news, and notes from around the denomination as it has sought to communicate the Good News to Cumberland Presbyterians throughout the world.

Even before the restructuring of the denominational leadership boards in 2007, the Board of Publications was no more. Its function, however, has been distributed over four different ministry teams (Discipleship, Pastoral Development, Missions, and Communications) which are responsible for the publica-tion and distribution of their own materials under the umbrella of the denomination.

The two remaining periodicals — **The CP Magazine** and **The Missionary Messenger**, fall under the care of the Communications Ministry Team, with the Missions Ministry Team providing content and edi-torial oversight for **The Missionary Messenger**.

Technologically, the publications have seen great changes. Each periodical has an online presence, and readers are able to subscribe digitally to the full-color, high-quality ma-terials.

In addition to new digital formats, the way Cumberland Presbyterians receive information has changed. The Communications Ministry Team, comprised of elected team members and staff members employed by the denomination, work together to communicate the message of the Cumberland Presbyterian church digitally through social media, email, websites, videos, and other platforms to a global audience.

"The Cumberland Presbyterian exists to inspire, equip, and engage readers in the work of Christian ministry."

— Mission Statement of **The Cumberland Presbyterian Magazine**

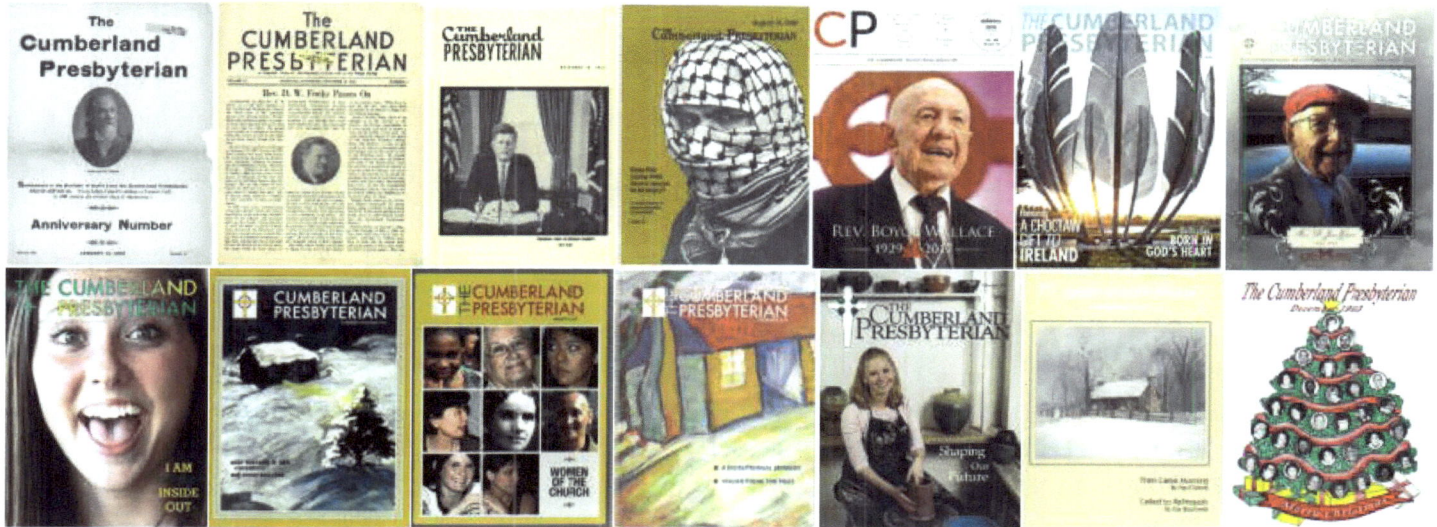

Above: Steven Shelton, Community Ministry Team leader, shows off the top of today's digital camera technology next to an older analog model. **At right:** Matthew H. Gore, the editor of *The Cumberland Presbyterian Magazine*, shows an issue from the 1960s featured in black and white next to an issue of the magazine from the 2010s, in full color and satin pages.

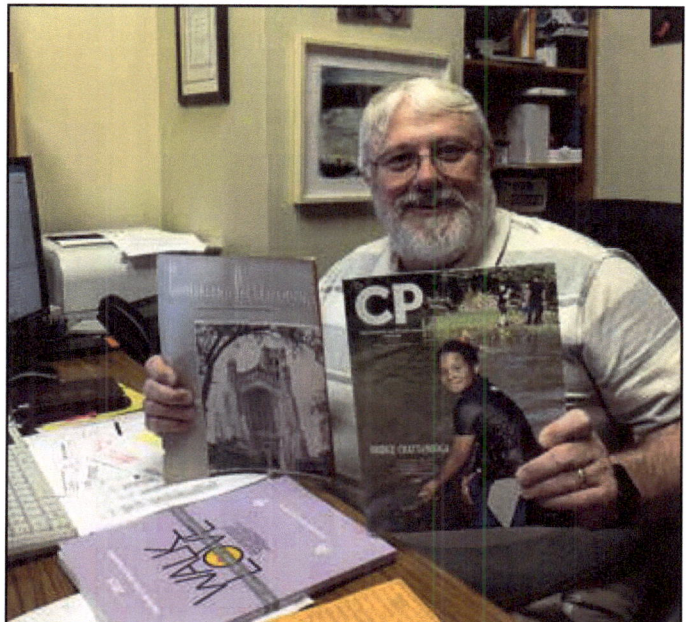

The High-Mark of Visual Arts

Since 1991, readers of *The Cumberland Presbyterian Magazine* or *The Missionary Messenger* haven't touched an issue without the imprint of Sowgand Sheikholeslami.

Sowgand is the senior art and creative director of the Cumberland Presbyterian Church, and artfully designs each issue of the denomination's periodicals, as well as other publications, fliers, and pamphlets. She helps each publication visually communicate its message and true meaning.

"I like things that make the reader really think about it, that are not obvious," Sowgand said. "You like to leave some of it to the person's imagination to fill in the gaps. You want them to have to digest it. You don't want to chew it up for them."

The Iranian native received her art degree in graphic design, and has spent a lifetime designing, illustrating, creating, and dreaming — all in bright colors. Each issue of the two main publications of the denomination almost always has an artistic element that is frame-worthy and original.

In fact, it's been largely due to Sowgand's pursuit, research, and negotiation that the *Messenger* and the *CP Mag* are received in beautiful full-color, satin page formats physically or high-definition products digitally. Quality, she believes, increases an individual's ability to communicate creatively.

That quality has come with new technology. Gone are the linotype machines popular even through the 20th century. Sowgand uses the latest pagination computer programs, digital photography, and commuicates with the printing house electronically.

She takes special pride in being able to take annual liturgical events that appear in the stories of the publications and think theologically around them to creative something new and vibrant each year. It's part of the joy and challenge of being an artist.

"How can I find my manna?," Sowgand says she asks herself each day. "I have to get up and look for it. There is some there. I will not be thirsty; I will be satisfied. It will fall in my lap."

Two of her favorite issues in the 2010s of the *CP Mag* have included liberal uses of the color yellow, and enjoys finding her inspiration in the submitted texts and articles of each publication.

"What I like is not necessarily what everyone else likes," the artist shrugged. "But there should be something that makes the reader think and wonder and see it in their own eyes and make it exciting."

Sowgand Sheikholeslami

SOURCES

1. Laurens Leurs, "The history of print from 1800 to 1849," *Prepressure,* Sept. 9, 2017, https://www.prepressure.com/printing/history/1800-1849.

2. Ben M. Barrus, Milton L. Baughn, and Thomas H. Campbell, *A People Called Cumberland Presbyterian* (Memphis, Tenn.: Frontier Press, 1972), 236.

3. Ibid.

4. Richard Beard, *Brief Biographical Sketches of Some of the Early Ministers of the Cumberland Presbyterian Church*, (Nashville, Tenn.: Southern Methodist Publishing House, 1867), 154-191.

5. Ben M. Barrus, Milton L. Baughn, and Thomas H. Campbell, *A People Called Cumberland Presbyterian* (Memphis, Tenn.: Frontier Press, 1972), 236.

6. "Subscription information," *The Religious and Literary Intelligencer* (Princeton, Ky.), Dec. 9, 1830.

7. Ben M. Barrus, Milton L. Baughn, and Thomas H. Campbell, *A People Called Cumberland Presbyterian* (Memphis, Tenn.: Frontier Press, 1972), 236.

8. Ibid.

9. Ben M. Barrus, Milton L. Baughn, and Thomas H. Campbell, *A People Called Cumberland Presbyterian* (Memphis, Tenn.: Frontier Press, 1972), 238.

10. Ibid.

11. Ibid.

12. B.W. McDonnold, *History of the Cumberland Presbyterian Church*, (Nashville, Tenn.: Board of Publication of the Cumberland Presbyterian Church, 1899), 586-587.

13. Richard Beard, *Brief Biographical Sketches of Some of the Early Ministers of the Cumberland Presbyterian Church*, (Nashville, Tenn.: Southern Methodist Publishing House, 1867), 339-355.

14. B.W. McDonnold, *History of the Cumberland Presbyterian Church*, (Nashville, Tenn.: Board of Publication of the Cumberland Presbyterian Church, 1899), 589.

15. Ibid.

16. Ibid, 590.

17. Ibid.

18. Ibid, 592.

19. Ben M. Barrus, Milton L. Baughn, and Thomas H. Campbell, *A People Called Cumberland Presbyterian* (Memphis, Tenn.: Frontier Press, 1972), 246.

20. *Minutes of the Forty-Fourth General Assembly of the Cumberland Presbyterian Church in the United States* (Nashville, Tenn.: Cumberland Presbyterian Board of Publication, 1874), 8.

21. Ibid, 18.

22. Ibid, 19-20.

23. Ben M. Barrus, Milton L. Baughn, and Thomas H. Campbell, *A People Called Cumberland Presbyterian* (Memphis, Tenn.: Frontier Press, 1972), 246.

24. *Minutes of the Forty-Fourth General Assembly of the Cumberland Presbyterian Church in the United States* (Nashville, Tenn.: Cumberland Presbyterian Board of Publication, 1874).

25. Ibid, 20.

26. Milton L. Baughn, *Social Views Reflected in*

Official Publications of the Cumberland Presbyterian Church 1875-1900 (Nashville, Tenn.: Vanderbilt University, thesis, 1954), 39.

27. Andy McClung, Lecture (Cumberland Presbyterian History and Doctrine course, Memphis Theological Seminary, Memphis, Tenn., Sept. 9, 2019)

28. Milton L. Baughn, *Social Views Reflected in Official Publications of the Cumberland Presbyterian Church 1875-1900* (Nashville, Tenn.: Vanderbilt University, thesis, 1954), 204-211.

29. I.W. Howerth, "Why Young Men Leave our Church," *The Cumberland Presbyterian* (Nashville, Tenn.), July 2, 1896.

30. *The Cumberland Banner*, (Jasper, Tenn.), Oct. 14, 1904.

31. Ibid.

32. R.L. Baskette, *History of Publication of the Cumberland Presbyterian Church* (Nashville, Tenn.: The Cumberland Press, 1810), 14.

33. "Change of Editors," *The Cumberland Presbyterian* (Nashville, Tenn.), March 3, 1910.

34. "The 50th Anniversary of The Cumberland Flag," *The Cumberland Flag* (Huntsville, Ala.), January 1981.

35. Andy McClung, Lecture (Cumberland Presbyterian History and Doctrine course, Memphis Theological Seminary, Memphis, Tenn., Sept. 23, 2019).

36. *Jubilee Journal* (Nashville, Tenn.: Women's Board of Missions), January 1930.

37. "Editorial," *The Missionary Messenger* (Louisville, Ky.: Women's Board of Missions), June 1931.

All documents used visually in this publication were reproduced digitally and retrieved from the Historical Archives of the Cumberland Presbyterian Church, online at www.cpcmc.org, or in the author's personal archives. Current-day photos are taken by the author. Photos of past editors of the *Cumberland Presbyterian* are reproductions of originals housed in the denominational archives, or provided by the Communications Ministry Team.